日本語擬態語辞典

五味太郎

講談社+α文庫

文庫版まえがき

　ちょうどその頃、つまりこの本を作った15年ほど前のことだけれど、ぼくのところにやや変わった外国人がなぜか多くやってきていた。ま、出版関係や美術関係のお仕事でやってきたのがほとんどなのだけれど、なかにはなんでやってきたのか今となっては思い出しようもないような人々もいた。
　たとえば合気道を研究しに日本に来たというイスラエル人だとか、日本料理に関してはぼくより数倍詳しいアメリカ人だとか。ただぼんやりよく遊びに来るインドネシア人だとか。知り合ったきっかけはいったいどんな具合だったのかよく判らないまま（判ったところで別にどうでもいいのだけれど）、なんとなく仲良くやっていたわけだ。

　で、イスラエル人はなにしろ合気道だし、アメリカ人はこれまた日本料理だから、当然の成り行きとして、ま、日本文化を語り合うことが多くなるわけだ。そしてインドネシア人はぼんやりしててもなにはともあれイスラーム教であるらしく、時間が来ると感心にも例のお祈りをしたりするのだ。西はどっちですか？　とかなんとかぼくに聞いたりして。
　だからお茶しながらもごく自然にイスラーム教と

仏教、あるいは他の宗教との比較論などに話がいくわけ。そう高尚なところまではお互いの実力ではいかないのだけれど。ま、軽い文化論というような具合で。

　それまでの外国人との付き合いというのはたぶん、こちらが出掛けていった先で、なんとなく適当に当地の言葉をこちらが操ってすませていたようなことが多かったわけだけれども、その頃からは立場がやや逆転して、それこそ適当に日本語を操りながらやってくるというような人物がやや増えたということなのだ。だからこちらもやや不足な部分はいい加減な英語などでごまかしながら、いちおうは日本語で会話をしていたわけだ。
　とはいえ、なにしろ彼らは通りすがりの観光客というのとは少し次元が違っていて、とりあえず文化交流的な付き合いだから、当然会話もやや高度になってくるわけで、そこであらためてぼくのほうが日本語の特性について意識せざるを得なくなってきたというわけだ。

　そしてそんな日常の意識をなんとなく本にするというぼくの仕事習慣のなかで、たとえば俳句について、あるいはことわざについてぼくなりのやり方で作業したわけだが、この日本語擬態語辞典もそんな流れのなかで作ったのだと思う。ぼくのなかであら

ためて日本語というものについての興味がわいてきていたのだろう。
　そしてその作業の着地点としてなんとなく意識していたのは、やはり彼らを含めた「日本語圏にぶらっとやってきた外国人のために」ということだったのかもしれない。初版当時のまえがきを今あらためて読むと、どうやらそんな気構えが充分にあったようだ。

　そしてその後も、日本語の教師になるためにやってきたフランス人だとか、日本人の亭主を探すためにとりあえず日本語を、なんていうアメリカ女性だとか、いろいろな次元で外国人がぼくのそばにやってきて、そのたびにこの日本語擬態語辞典がひっかかってきたりはするのだけれど、たとえば「にやにや」は「near near」というわけ？　なんて聞かれたりして、まだ学問の着地点はほとんど見出せてはいないわけだ。
　文庫版化のせめてもの必然性か。

2004年6月

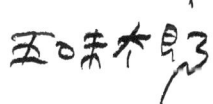

まえがき

　たとえば、歌舞伎とか文楽とか、あるいは茶道とか華道なんてものがぼくはわりあいに好きで、それなりの造詣も愛着もあるのですが、それらをひとたび「我が日本の誇るべき文化」というような視点でとらえることを好みません。むしろ嫌います。その視点で外国人に向って伝えたくもありませんし、同胞諸氏と再確認しあいたくもまたありません。まして誇らし気に説明し理解を求めたり、同意を促したりする気にもなりません。

　すべてそういった類のものが身近にあってね、たとえば歌舞伎にしたって、あえていえばある種の日本人が編み出した芝居のひとつの形式で、ま、それが案外洒落ていて、ぼくの好みに合うんだよね、という程度のとらえ方で、華道に造詣も愛着も深いといったところで、その本質は少しでっち上げが過ぎていて、相当屁理屈が多いねと見ているわけで、結構きびしく客観的にもとらえているわけです。

　けれど、ぼくのネイティブなものに対する文化観がこと「日本語における擬態語」というものに対した時にだけ、やや狂います。突然、誇らしく自慢

Preface

Traditional arts like kabuki, bunraku, tea ceremony, and flower arrangement give me quite a lot of pleasure, and I do have a certain degree of knowledge of and affection for them. But I do not like to consider these arts as examples of Japanese culture of which I should be proud. In fact, I very much dislike looking at them from this angle. I feel no desire at all to introduce these arts to outsiders or to share my feelings about them with other Japanese. I certainly have no wish to proudly show them off and promote understanding and approval of them.

These arts were a part of my environment when I grew up, that is all. I like kabuki simply because it is quite witty, which suits my taste. I also have some knowledge of and affection for flower arrangement, but I confess that I sometimes find this art a little too artificial and forced. You see, I look at my native culture with a very critical and objective eye.

When it comes to onomatopoeic expressions in Japanese, however, my cool attitude changes

し、説明して理解を促し、同意を得たくなります。ネイティブなものといえば、言語ほどネイティブなものはないわけですから、自らの母国語であるところの日本語そのものを誇らしく思うのが世の常なのでしょうが、何故かやはり、その気がぼくには起りません。それもまた歌舞伎と同じように、いやそれ以上に生まれた時から身近にそんなものがあってね、なんとなくぼくもそれを使って暮してきたわけで、特に誇らしくも、自慢すべきことのようにも思われません。

愛着ゆえだけで誇るなら、それはよくある故郷自慢、家族自慢と同じレベルの、ただ我がままでありましょうし、やや客観的に日本語をとらえたところで、それが果して言語としてどの程度の完成度なのか、論理的にゆるぎないものなのか、はたまた、思考するための有効な手段たり得るのか、などなどという判断はつきかねます。判断すべき立場にもおりません。

ですから、日本語そのものを特に外国の方々におすすめする気にはなりません。喋りたければお喋りなさい、読み書きしたくばどうぞおやり下さい、という程度。もちろん、相当むずかしいからおやめになった方が賢明ですよなどとも言いません。

dramatically. I suddenly become very proud and boastful and have a burning desire to introduce them and get people to understand them. Since language is the most native part of a native culture, it is no doubt normal for Japanese people to be proud of the Japanese language. For some reason, however, I do not feel such pride at all. Like kabuki, indeed even more so, the Japanese language has been with me since the day I was born. I grew up with it, but I do not feel any special pride in it.

If affection is the only reason for being proud, then this is just the same as people boasting about their hometown or their family. It is no more than egoism. Even if I try to look at the Japanese language objectively, I am not in a position to judge how perfect it is as a language, whether it is logically sound or whether it serves as an effective vehicle for thoughts.

So I have no special desire to recommend the Japanese language itself to foreigners. If they want to speak it, fine. If they want to read and write it, that is fine too. Of course, I am not going to advise people to give up because it is too difficult, either.

しかし、「日本語における擬態語」というやつをぼくは外国人諸氏に心からおすすめします。「歌舞伎」も「すきやき」も「天ぷら」もとりたててすすめないこのぼくが、「擬態語」をいちどお試しになってみたらいかがですか、という気合いでおすすめする。つまりそれがこの本なのでありますが。

　それはどうやら、この「日本語における擬態語」というものの存在が、日本語の中のひとつの要素、ひとつの品詞といったような、たとえばあまたの料理の中の天ぷら、演劇の中のひとつの形式、様式としての歌舞伎といった在り様とは根本的に違ったレベルのものだとぼくが考えているからなのです。

　極端にいえば、これは本当に言葉なのかしら、とぼくは未だに迷い疑っているのです。その迷いと疑いの原因のひとつとして、品詞が決定できない、文法上、文章法上の確たる品詞として、この擬態語をとらえ切れない、ということがあります。無責任な言語学者はただ「日本語に多くの擬態語あり」で済ませていますし、少し賢い学者はこの言葉群が表面的にもつ幼稚性、非論理性等を理由に、あまり深く言及いたしません。

　つまり本気には扱わないのです。扱えないといった方が正しいでしょう。それも無理はないな、とぼ

But while I do not especially recommend foreigners to try kabuki, or sukiyaki, or tempura, I have no hesitation in recommending them to try Japanese onomatopoeic expressions. This is why I set about compiling this book.

Kabuki is one form of Japanese drama, and tempura is one type of Japanese cuisine, but onomatopoeic expressions are much more than just one part of the Japanese language.

I often wonder whether onomatopoeic expressions are really words, because grammatically they cannot be defined as any specific part of speech. Lazy linguists usually skip over the topic by saying something like "the Japanese language has a large number of onomatopoeic expressions." And more diligent linguists only touch on them briefly because, they say, onomatopoeic expressions are childish and illogical.

So linguists do not deal with onomatopoeic expressions. Or perhaps, I should say, they are unable to deal with them. And this is not surprising, onomatopoeic expressions are not the kind of subject matter that expert linguists can take up as

くは考えます。これは、とても専門家の言語学者が分化した学問として扱えるような代物ではないのです。だって、そもそもこれは言語ではないんですから。敢えていえば「言語の素」みたいなものなのです。言語のカオス、カオス状態の言語、それこそ、もやもや、どろどろ、ごちゃごちゃ、ばらばら、ふわふわ、などと擬態語そのものをもってしか表現し得ないような、さて、これから必要とあらば言語にでもなりましょうか、とゆったりとくくっているような状態の言葉群なのですから、かしこい、ただしい、えらい、あるいは立派な、というような、ゆるぎない形容詞、形容動詞等をもって表現し得るような人々にはなかなか扱えません。下手に扱うとエライ目にあいます。

　ぼくぐらいが扱うのが丁度いいのです。なにしろぼくは、もやもや、どろどろ、ごちゃごちゃ、そして、ぐだぐだ、へらへら、うろうろ、の専門家ですからね。

　そしてさらに、けっして日本語の専門家たり得ない、つまり日本語をネイティブ・ランゲージにしていない人々こそ、この言葉群を扱える有資格者です。そしてたとえば、動物学者が、観察し、捕獲し、研究し、分類し、と懸命にアプローチしたところで、当の動物はほとんどそれには無頓着に勝手

a separate topic and study academically. After all, onomatopoeic expressions are not really language; they are, in a sense, raw language. *Moya moya, doro doro, gocha gocha, bara bara, fuwa fuwa* — no other words can describe these expressions. They represent a world of their own — a group of expressions on the verge of becoming words if necessary. Linguists, who are always described by such orthodox adjectives as *kashikoi* (wise), *tadashii* (right), *erai* (great), or *rippana* (respected), cannot handle them. If they handle them carelessly, they will run into problems.

Onomatopoeic expressions are just right for a person like myself, because I am a specialist when it comes to being *moya moya, doro doro,* and *gocha gocha,* not to mention *guda guda, hera hera,* and *uro uro.*

You do not have to be an expert in the Japanese language to appreciate these expressions; indeed, non-native speakers are probably even more qualified to handle them than Japanese linguists. In the same way as animals go on living quite indifferently while zoologists zestfully observe, capture, study, and classify them, words go on living despite the

に生きているのと同じように、言葉も学問的な管理にはほとんどなじまず、それこそ生き物そのものでありますから、勝手気ままに生きてゆくわけであります。それが動物、それが言葉、そんな、ま、当り前のことを改めて思い起させてくれるような力がこの「日本語における擬態語」というものには確実にあります。

　ですから、この言葉の世界を楽しく味わっていただけたら、日本語そのものの理解というよりはむしろ、言葉とは何かというような、やや壮大なテーマが案外気楽に考察できるのではないかと思います。それになにはともあれ、これは日本語には違いないのであり、さらに「日本語の素」なのですから、このままでもすぐにお使いになれますし、ちょっと手を加えていただけたら、立派な一品にもなるはずです。ぼくはすきやき、天ぷらより、「擬態語」をおすすめします。お試し下さい。

五味太郎

efforts of scholars to manage them. Onomatopoeic expressions remind us of this natural state of affairs.

If you enjoy the world of onomatopoeic expressions, I think they will help you understand something about not so much the Japanese language itself as the somewhat grandeur topic of the nature of words. And of course, these expressions are part of the Japanese language; indeed, they are raw Japanese, so you will be able to use them as they are. And if you add a little more, you will be speaking wonderful Japanese. I do not necessarily recommend sukiyaki or tempura, but I do suggest you try these onomatopoeic expressions. I am sure you will relish them.

GOMI TARO

AN ILLUSTRATED DICTIONARY
OF JAPANESE ONOMATOPOEIC EXPRESSIONS

日本語擬態語辞典

見出し語と語源が同じ、あるいは何らかの因果関係があると思われる言葉（〈例〉うきうき―浮く　しずしず―静かだ）については、意味の最後に☆印をつけて記した。

   Words that have the same root as the onomatopoeic expression or some other close connection with it, such as *uku* for *uki uki* and *shizukada* for *shizu shizu*, are included after a ☆ mark following the explanation.

atsu atsu
Describes something that looks piping hot. Also used to describe a couple who are head over heels in love. ☆*atsui*

あつあつ
見るからに熱い様子。男女の仲がとてもよい様子にも用いる。☆熱い

appu appu
あっぷあっぷ

appu appu
Describes someone floundering in water and almost drowning. Also used to describe someone in trouble or difficulty. In deep water.

あっぷあっぷ
おぼれかけて、もがいているさま。とても困って苦しんでいる様子にも用いる。

iki iki
Describes someone or something that is full of life. Lifelike. Vivid. ☆*ikiru*

いきいき
元気、活気がある様子。生きがいいさま。☆生きる

iji iji
Describes someone unable to be honest or frank in front of others. Also describes reserved, timid, or servile behavior or attitude. Cowardly. ☆*ijikeru*

いじいじ
素直に人に対することができず、行動や態度がはっきりしないさま。卑屈な様子。☆いじける

iso iso
Describes someone who moves as if full of joy or expectation. Cheerfully. Excitedly.

いそいそ
喜びや期待で、動作が調子づく様子。

ichi ichi
One by one. In detail. Persistently. ☆*ichi*

いちいち
ひとつひとつ。細大もらさず。しつこく。☆一（いち）

iya iya　いやいや

iya iya
Reluctantly. With a heavy heart. ☆*iyada*

いやいや
いやだが、しかたなく。☆いやだ

iyo iyo
①At last. ②Even more. ③Without doubt; decidedly. ④The final stage of something.

いよいよ
①ついに。②今までよりいっそう。③確かに。決定的に。
④極限の状態。

ira ira
Describes someone who is irritated or angry because things are not going as desired.

いらいら
思いどおりにならないため、あせって落ち着かず、腹立たしいさま。

uki uki
Describes someone who is happy and excited. In a buoyant mood. ☆*uku*

うきうき
うれしくて、心がはずむ様子。浮かれるさま。☆浮く

uji uji
Hesitant, irresolute. Used to describe someone who wants to do something but cannot bring himself or herself to do it.

うじうじ
態度がはっきりしない様子。何かをしたいと思いながら決断がつかずにいるさま。

uja uja
Describes many small things gathered together and moving, such as a swarm of insects or a crowd of people seen from a distance.

うじゃうじゃ
小さな虫などがたくさん集まってうごめいているさま。

uzu uzu
Describes someone itching to do something.
☆*uzuku*

うずうず
何かがしたくてたまらず、落ち着かない様子。☆うずく

uda uda
①Describes someone who is slow and lazy. Idle.
②Describes someone saying something meaningless in a drawn-out manner.

うだうだ
①てきぱき行動せず、怠惰に過ごす様子。②無意味なことをくどく言うさま。

uto uto
Describes someone dozing. Napping.

うとうと
いねむりしている様子。もっぱら、眠る形容に用いる。

uro uro
Describes someone wandering about aimlessly or someone who has lost sight of their goal. Loafing around. Hanging around.

うろうろ
あてもなく、または目的を見失って、あたりをさまよう様子。

ozu ozu

Describes behaving in a fearful or diffident manner. Gingerly. ☆*ozu (ojiru)*

おずおず
恐れながら、あるいは遠慮がちに行動する様子。☆おず（おじる）

ota ota
Describes someone who is too surprised or shocked to respond properly.

おたおた
驚きあわてて、まともに何もできないでいる様子。

odo odo おどおど

odo odo
Describes someone who is restless with fear or uncertainty. Cowering.

おどおど
恐れや不安で落ち着かない様子。

oro oro
Describes someone who is confused and does not know what to do. Flustered.

おろおろ
どうしていいかわからず、とり乱すさま。

gaku gaku
①Describes something that was fixed in place but comes loose and begins moving, such as a loose tooth. ②Describes part of the body trembling.

がくがく
①固定してあったものがゆるんで動く様子。②体の一部が小刻みに震えるさま。

kachi kachi
①Describes the sound made when solid objects hit each other. ②Describes something very hard. Also used to describe someone's strait-laced views or to describe a person who is stiff with nervous tension. Rigid.

かちかち
①硬いものがぶつかり合う音。②とても堅いさま。人の考え方が堅苦しい様子や、緊張などで体が硬くなっている様子にも用いられる。

gatsu gatsu (がつがつ)

Describes someone eating greedily. Also used to describe someone who hungers after something. Craving.

がつがつ
むさぼり食うさま。何かを貪欲に求める様子にも用いる。

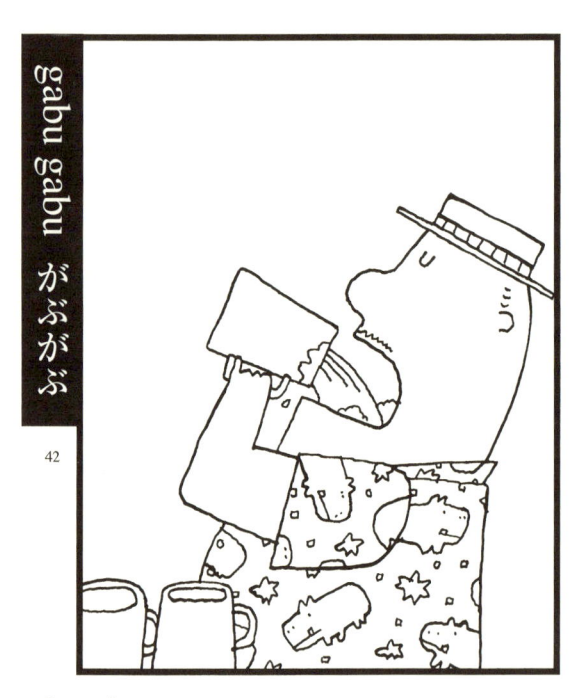

gabu gabu
Describes someone downing a large drink thirstily. Gulping down. Guzzling.

がぶがぶ
大量の液体を勢いよく飲む様子。

gami gami
Describes someone nagging. Griping.

がみがみ
口やかましく文句を言うさま。

gaya gaya
Describes a noisy situation, with many people speaking at the same time. Hubbub.

がやがや
大勢の話し声が響いて騒がしい様子。

kan kan
①Describes someone who is very angry. In a rage.
②Describes the burning sun or burning coal.
③Describes the clanging sound made when metal or other hard objects hit each other.

かんかん
①激怒する様子。②太陽が強く照りつけるさま。炭がさかんに燃えているさま。③金属など硬いものがぶつかって出る、高く澄んだ音。

gisu gisu / ぎすぎす

gisu gisu
①Describes a relationship or an atmosphere that lacks friendliness. Strained. ②Describes someone who is thin and bony.

ぎすぎす
①親しみやゆとりがないさま。②やせて骨ばった様子。

kibi kibi きびきび

kibi kibi
Describes attitude, behavior, or speech that is prompt, businesslike, and alert.

きびきび
態度・言動が敏速で無駄がなく、小気味よい様子。

gyū gyū

①Describes the sound of crinkling leather or a creaking door. ②Describes pushing, packing, or closing something as strongly or tightly as possible. ③Describes bringing someone to their knees by severely reproaching or drilling them.

ぎゅうぎゅう
①物がこすれたり、きしんだりして出る鈍い音。革製品がこすれる音など。②余裕がなくなるほど強く力を加えるさま。押す、詰める、締めるなどの形容に用いる。③強く責めたり鍛えたりして、まいらせる様子。

kyoro kyoro
Describes someone looking around restlessly. Staring about.

きょろきょろ
落ち着きなく、あたりを見回すさま。

gira gira
Describes something shining brightly. Dazzlingly. Also used to describe a person's appearance or look. Glaring.

ぎらぎら
強く輝く様子。どぎつく光るさま。態度、視線などにも用いる。

gui gui
Describes doing something forcefully and continuously, such as gulping down a drink or pulling someone by the hand.

ぐいぐい
力強く、連続して何かを行う様子。飲む、引っ張るなどの形容に用いる。

kusa kusa くさくさ

kusa kusa
Describes someone who is feeling depressed because something unpleasant has happened. Feeling blue. ☆*kusaru*

くさくさ
いやなことがあって、気分が晴れないさま。☆腐る

guzu guzu
①Describes sluggish, dillydallying behavior. ②Describes something that is uncertain, such as the weather. ③Describes someone who is grumbling or complaining. ④Describes something that has lost its shape. Loose. ☆*guzuda*

ぐずぐず
①行動が敏速でないさま。②(天気など)様子がはっきりしないさま。③不平を言うさま。④形がくずれて、しまりがないさま。☆ぐずだ

kuta kuta くたくた

54

kuta kuta
Describes something that is withered. Also used to describe someone who is very tired. Worn-out. Exhausted.

くたくた
張りがなく、しおれた様子。とても疲れた様子にも用いる。

gucha gucha

①Describes something soft and soggy. Also describes the action of stirring or mashing such a substance. ②Describes something in awful disarray. Higgledy-piggledy. ③Describes grumbling.

ぐちゃぐちゃ
①水分をたっぷり含んで柔らかい様子。または、水分を含んだものをかき回したりつぶしたりする様子。②ひどく乱れた様子。③ぐちっぽく、あれこれ言う様子。

kudo kudo
Describes saying the same thing over and over again. ☆*kudoi*

くどくど
同じことをしつこく繰り返して言うさま。☆くどい

kune kune   くねくね

kune kune
Describes something that curves gently several times. Meandering. Also used to describe someone wriggling his or her body. ☆*kuneru*

くねくね
何度もゆるやかに曲がるさま。また、体をよじるさまにも用いる。☆くねる

kuyo kuyo くよくよ

kuyo kuyo
Describes worrying for ages about a trivial matter. Moping. Brooding.

くよくよ
ささいなことをいつまでも気に病む様子。

kura kura
Describes having a dizzy spell. Feeling giddy.

くらくら
目まいがして、倒れそうな様子。

kuru kuru
①Describes a small object spinning lightly. ②Describes quickly winding up a long object, such as string. ③Describes someone who is quick at moving or coming up with ideas. ④Describes a situation in which changes are kaleidoscopic.

くるくる
①連続して軽快に回転する様子。②長いものを手早く幾重にも巻きつけるさま。③動作や頭の回転が早くて活発な様子。④変化がめまぐるしいさま。

guru guru ぐるぐる

61

guru guru
①Describes something spinning round and round.
②Describes winding something round and round or rolling something up. ③Describes moving something again and again.

ぐるぐる
①連続して回転する様子。②幾重にも巻きつけるさま。
③次々に移動させる様子。

gun gun
Describes something progressing or growing very rapidly.

ぐんぐん
力強く、進み方がめざましいさま。

kechi kechi
Describes someone who is stingy with money or other things. Tightfisted. ☆*kechida*

けちけち
お金や品物をいかにも惜しそうにするさま。☆けちだ

keba keba けばけば

keba keba
Describes someone or something that is gaudy. Garish. ☆*kebakebashii*

けばけば
派手でどぎついさま。☆けばけばしい

gera gera げらげら

gera gera
Describes laughing in a noisy, uncontrolled manner. Guffawing loudly.

げらげら
大声で、しまりなく笑うさま。もっぱら、笑う形容に用いる。

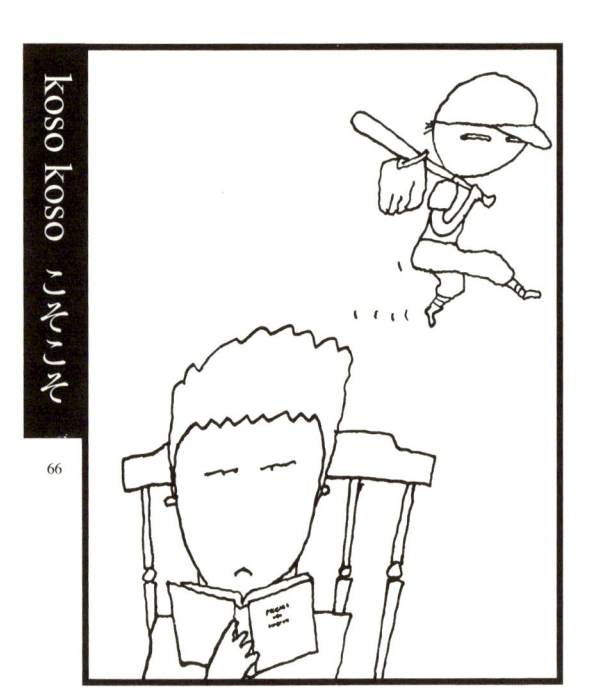

koso koso
Describes stealthy movement to avoid being discovered by others. Like a thief in the night.

こそこそ
人に知られないように、ひそかに行う様子。

goso goso
Describes a jarring sound or something that makes such a sound. The sound of rummaging.

ごそごそ
耳ざわりな音がするさま。また、そういう音を立てて動き回るさま。

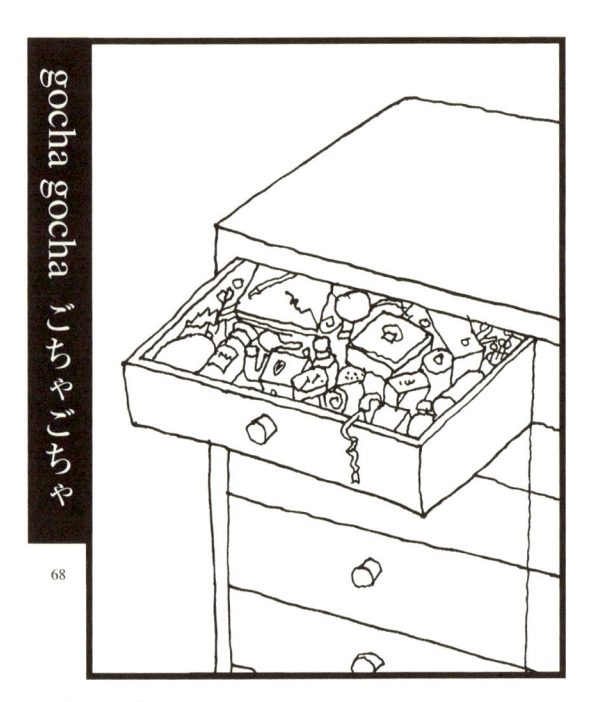

gocha gocha
①Describes a jumble. ②Describes someone complaining about one thing and another.

ごちゃごちゃ
①多くの物が入り乱れて、雑然とした様子。②あれこれ不平不満を言い立てるさま。

kotsu kotsu

①Describes the sound of a hard object hitting something, such as shoes hitting the pavement or someone knocking at a door. Tapping. Clicking. Drumming. ②Describes someone grinding away at their job. Unflaggingly.

こつこつ
①硬いものが打ち当たって発する音。舗道を歩く靴音、ノックの音など。②地道な努力を続けるさま。

koro koro

①Describes something small and round rolling over. ②Describes a high, clear, pleasant sound, such as the ringing of a bell or a young girl's giggle. ③Describes something fat and round. ④Describes something, such as the topic of conversation, that changes frequently.

ころころ
①小さく丸いものがころがるさま。②高く澄んで、響きのよい音。鈴の音、若い女性の笑い声などの形容に用いる。③太って、いかにも丸いさま。④ある状態に、たやすく何度も至る様子。話が変わるなどの形容に用いる。

kowa gowa
Describes nervous, frightened behavior. With trepidation. ☆*kowai*

こわごわ
こわがりながら行うさま。☆こわい

gowa gowa ごわごわ

gowa gowa
Describes something that has become stiff, such as paper or cloth.

ごわごわ
紙、布などが硬くこわばった様子。

zā zā

①Describes the sound of rushing water. Often used to describe the sound of pouring rain. ②Describes the sound of static on television or loudspeakers.

ざあざあ

①水が勢いよく流れる音。とくに、雨が激しく降る音の形容によく用いる。②テレビ、スピーカーなどの雑音。

zaku zaku
①Describes a large number of metal coins or jewels.
②Describes the sound of chopping vegetables or the like. Also describes cutting something roughly.
③Describes the sound of gravel or the like being mixed. ④Describes the sound of walking over gravel or frost.

ざくざく
①金貨、宝石などがたくさんある様子。②野菜などを切り刻む音。また、切り方が粗いさま。③粗い粒状のものが混ざり合う音。④砂利や霜柱などを踏んで歩く音。

saba saba
①Describes the feeling of relief one has after settling an irritating or unpleasant matter. Getting a load off one's mind. ②Describes someone who is plain-spoken. Candid. ☆*sabaku*

さばさば
①面倒なことやいやなことが片づいて、すっきりした様子。
②性格がさっぱりしているさま。☆さばく

samu zamu
Describes a cold, bleak scene. Wintry. Desolate.
☆*samui*

さむざむ
いかにも寒そうなさま。殺風景な様子。☆寒い

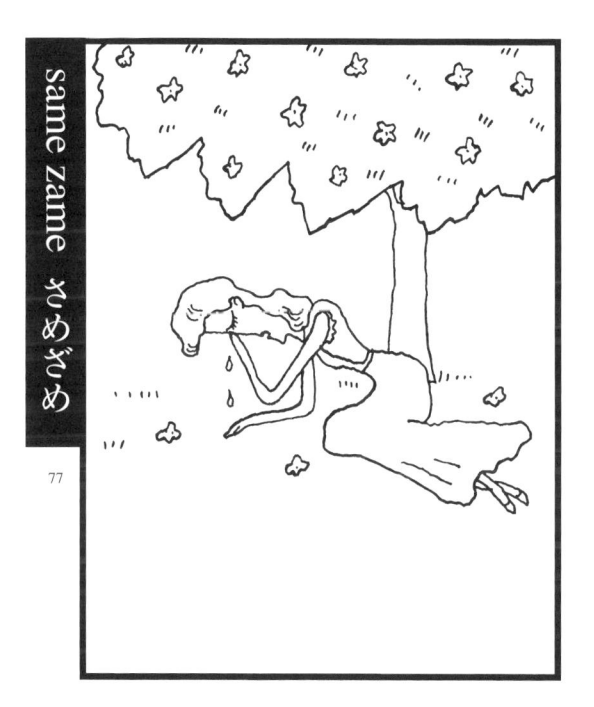

same zame

Describes someone crying bitterly. Broken-heartedly. Sorrowfully.

さめざめ

涙を流し、しのび泣くさま。もっぱら、泣く形容に用いる。

shiku shiku
①Describes someone weeping. Sobbing.
②Describes a dull pain. Often used to describe stomachache or toothache.

しくしく
①静かに泣き続けるさま。②鈍い痛みが続くさま。腹痛や歯痛の形容に用いる。

shige shige
①Describes taking a close look. Scrutinizing.
②Describes visiting a place frequently.

しげしげ
①よく観察する様子。②頻繁に通うさま。

shizu shizu
Describes someone acting or moving quietly. Gracefully. ☆*shizukada*

しずしず
静かに行動するさま。しとやかな様子。☆静かだ

jito jito じとじと

jito jito
Describes an unpleasantly hot and damp atmosphere. Sweaty.

じとじと
暑くて湿気や水分が多く、不快なさま。汗ばむ様子。

shibu shibu
Describes doing something reluctantly. Grudgingly.
☆*shiburu*

しぶしぶ
やむを得ず。気が進まないが、しかたなく。☆渋る

shimi jimi
①Describes feeling something deeply. ②Describes doing something quietly. Calmly. ☆*shimiru*

しみじみ
①身にしみて感じるさま。②心静かに、落ち着いて行う様子。☆しみる

shā shā

shā shā
Describes someone remaining unmoved despite having done something deserving reproach. Brazenfacedly. Shamelessly.

しゃあしゃあ
非難されるべきことをしながら、平気でいる様子。あつかましいさま。

jabu jabu
Describes the sound and action of splashing water.

じゃぶじゃぶ
水をはね飛ばすときに出る音。また、その様子。

jiri jiri じりじり

①Describes someone running out of patience and fretting. ②Describes something that draws closer little by little. ③Describes the scorching sun. ④Describes something that has been burned. ⑤Describes the sound of an alarm bell.

じりじり
①待ち切れず、じれる様子。②少しずつ、迫るように進む様子。③直射日光が照りつけるさま。④焼け焦げるさま。⑤ベルなどが鳴る音。

jiro jiro
Describes someone staring rudely.

じろじろ
無遠慮に見つめるさま。もっぱら、見る形容に用いる。

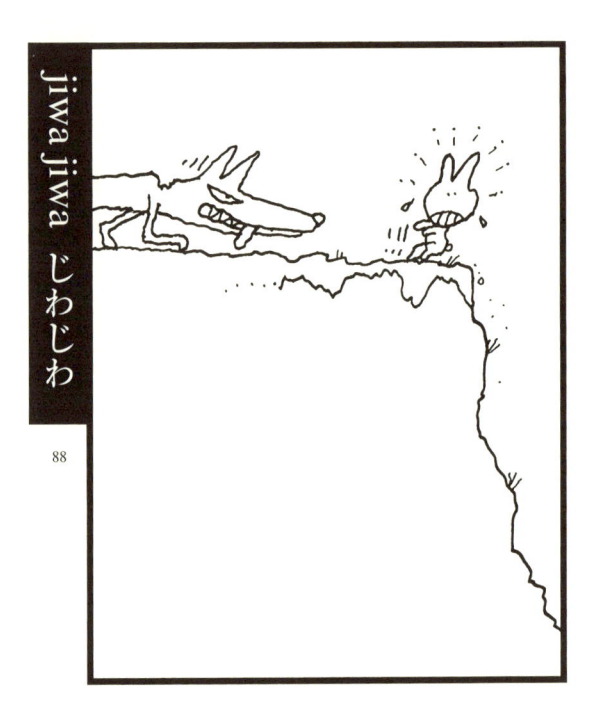

jiwa jiwa
Describes something advancing slowly but steadily.

じわじわ
物事が、ゆっくりではあるが確実に進んでいく様子。

sui sui すいすい

sui sui
Describes moving smoothly and easily through something, such as someone swimming gracefully or a car moving swiftly along an empty street.

すいすい
水面などを軽やかに進む様子。乗り物などが滞りなく進むさま。

zuka zuka
Describes someone making an entrance boldly or rudely.

ずかずか
無遠慮に入り込むさま。もっぱら、入り込む、踏み込むなどの形容に用いる。

zuki zuki

ずきずき

Describes a throbbing pain, including heartbreak.

傷が脈打つように、絶えず強く痛むさま。心の痛みにも用いる。

suku suku すくすく

suku suku
Describes growing healthily and steadily.

すくすく
すこやかに、順調に伸び育つ様子。

zuke zuke
Describes speaking bluntly. Brusquely.

ずけずけ
無遠慮に、はっきりとものを言う様子。

sugo sugo
Describes leaving a place in low spirits. Dejectedly.

すごすご
気落ちして、元気なくその場を立ち去るさま。もっぱら、立ち去る、帰るなど、その場から離れる形容に用いる。

zuta zuta
Describes something torn. Ragged. Also used to describe a deeply broken heart.

ずたずた
細かく切れたり裂けたりしたさま。心が深く傷ついた形容にも用いる。

suya suya
Describes sleeping peacefully. Soundly.

すやすや
やすらかに眠っている様子。もっぱら、眠る形容に用いる。

sura sura
Describes something proceeding smoothly. Without a hitch. Often used to describe eloquent speech or writing.

すらすら
動作または物事が、よどみなく順調に進むさま。話す、書くなどの形容によく用いる。

zuru zuru
①Describes the sound or act of dragging. Also describes the sound made by someone slurping food. ②Describes something that is loose. ③Describes an undesirable situation that drags on inconclusively.

ずるずる
①物を引きずったり、すすったりする音や様子。②しまりがないさま。③けじめがつかず、望ましくない状態が長びく様子。

sure sure
Describes being extremely close. Also used to describe something that has almost reached or exceeded the limit. On the verge of.

すれすれ
非常に接近しているさま。また、もう少しで限度を越えそうな様子にも用いる。

seka seka
Describes someone who acts impetuously. Hastily.
☆*sekasu*

せかせか
動作や態度が落ち着かず、気ぜわしいさま。☆せかす

zoku zoku

①Describes a feeling of chilliness. ②Describes someone who is so tense or excited that their body trembles or a chill runs down their spine. Expresses fear, anticipation, joy, or emotion. ※ A homonym of this word describes something continuing without interruption.

ぞくぞく
①寒けを感じるさま。②体が震えたり背筋に寒けを感じたりするほど、緊張したり興奮したりするさま。恐怖、期待、喜び、感動などを表す。※べつに、途切れることなく続くさまを表す同音異義語「ぞくぞく（続々）」あり。

soro soro そろそろ

soro soro
①Describes doing something slowly and quietly.
②Describes a situation or time that is approaching. Before long.

そろそろ
①ゆっくり、静かに行うさま。②ある状態や時期になりかかった様子。まもなく。

zoro zoro

①Describes a large number of people or things standing in line. ②Describes trailing a skirt or the like in a slovenly way.

ぞろぞろ
①人や物がたくさん並んで続く様子。②着物のすそなどを、だらしなく引きずるさま。

sowa sowa
Describes someone who is nervously excited about something.

そわそわ
何かに気を取られて、落ち着かないさま。

taji taji
たじたじ

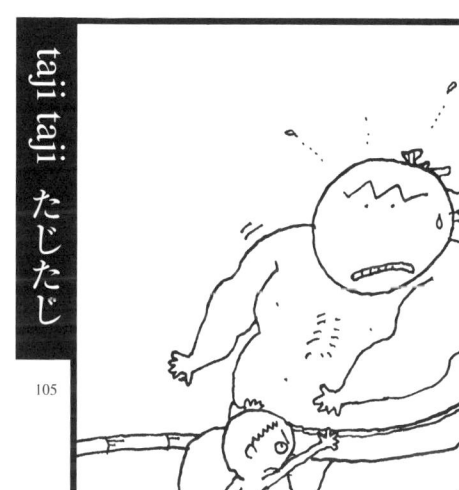

taji taji
Describes someone retreating, overwhelmed by the power of another. Recoiling. Flinching. Cringing.
☆*tajirogu*

たじたじ
相手の力や勢いに圧倒されて、あとずさりする様子。ひるむさま。☆たじろぐ

dabu dabu　だぶだぶ

dabu dabu
Describes clothing that is too big. Loose. Baggy.

だぶだぶ
衣服などが大きすぎて、体に合わないさま。

tara tara

①Describes water or any other liquid that is dripping. ②Describes endless complaining or boasting.

たらたら
①液体がしたたり落ちるさま。②文句、自慢など、いい加減にやめてほしいことを際限なく言う様子。

dara dara
①Describes water or any other liquid that is streaming. ②Describes something that goes on for a long time without conclusion. Also describes dilatory behavior. Dillydallying. ③Describes a long, gentle slope.

だらだら
①液体が流れ出るさま。②長々と続いて、しまりがない様子。また、動作が緩慢なさま。③ゆるやかな傾斜が続くさま。

chiku chiku ちくちく

chiku chiku
Describes a sharp object pricking something and also the pain felt from such a prick.

ちくちく
先のとがったもので、小刻みに刺す様子。また、そのような痛みを感じるさま。

chibi chibi
Describes doing something little by little to make it last as long as possible. For example, sipping a drink. ☆*chibiru*

ちびちび
もったいなさそうに、ちょっとずつ。☆ちびる

choko choko
①Describes walking or running with short steps. Toddling. Hobbling. ②Describes someone who is restless and constantly on the move. ③Describes getting something done easily without much time or effort.

ちょこちょこ
①小股で早歩きしたり走ったりするさま。②落ち着かず、たえず動き回っている様子。③時間や手間をかけず、物事を簡単にすませる様子。

chira chira ちらちら

chira chira
①Describes something small and light drifting down. Fluttering. ②Describes a light that flickers or appears to flicker. ③Describes something that is seen or heard intermittently. Also used to describe someone casting glances at something.

ちらちら
①小さく軽いものがひるがえりながら落ちるさま。②光が小刻みに明滅するさま。また、そのように感じるさま。③断続して見えたり聞こえたりする様子。視線を何度かすばやく走らせるさまにも用いる。

tsuka tsuka つかつか

tsuka tsuka
Describes heading straight for a destination without any hesitation. Walking briskly. Marching.

つかつか
ためらわずに進み出るさま。もっぱら、歩み寄るなど、目的に向かっていく形容に用いる。

tsuya tsuya つやつや

tsuya tsuya
Describes a shining surface. Glossy. Glistening. Sheeny. ☆*tsuya*

つやつや
表面に光沢があって美しいさま。☆つや

tsuru tsuru

①Describes a smooth surface. Polished. Also describes slipping on a smooth surface. ②Describes the sound made by someone slurping noodles.

つるつる
①表面がなめらかなさま。また、なめらかなものに触れてすべるさま。②麺類をすする音。

tsun tsun

①Describes someone being prim and unsociable. Aloof. Describes someone being sullen and morose. ②Describes something pointed, or something pointed that is growing. ③Describes a sharp smell.

つんつん
①とりすまして取っつきにくいさま。機嫌が悪く無愛想な様子。②先がとがった様子。また、とがったものが伸びるさま。③刺激的な臭いが鼻をつくさま。

teku teku てくてく

teku teku
Describes walking quite a distance at a steady pace.

てくてく
かなりの距離を地道に歩き続ける様子。もっぱら、歩く形容に用いる。

dere dere

Describes a loose attitude or appearance. Often used to describe a man's spoony attitude toward a woman.

でれでれ
態度、身なりなどにしまりがない様子。とくに、男性が女性に対してだらしない態度をとる形容に多く用いる。

doki doki
Describes a pounding heart. Palpitating. Beating fast.

どきどき
心臓が激しく鼓動する音や様子。

tobo tobo
Describes walking wearily. Trudging.

とぼとぼ
元気なく歩く様子。もっぱら、歩く形容に用いる。

doro doro
①Describes something covered in mud. ②Describes a liquid that is opaque and sticky. Syrupy. ③Describes mixed emotions. Muddled. ☆*doro*

どろどろ
①泥がたくさんついたさま。②液体が不透明で粘りけが強いさま。③感情などが複雑に絡んで、すっきりしない状態。
☆泥

ton ton
①Describes the sound of gentle knocking or of someone going up or down the stairs. Tapping. Clip-clop. ②Describes something going well. ③Describes two things that are just about the same. Even. Often used to describe equal gain and loss.

とんとん
①軽く打ち当たる音が連続するさま。ノックや階段を上り下りする音など。②物事が順調に運ぶ様子。③二つの物事がだいたい同じで差がない様子。とくに、損得が同じ場合の形容によく用いる。

don don どんどん

don don
①Describes a continuous loud sound like the beating of a drum or someone stamping their feet on the floor. ②Describes something that proceeds steadily or someone going ahead with something without hesitation.

どんどん
①力強く打ち当たる音が連続するさま。太鼓の音、床を踏み鳴らす音など。②物事が滞ることなく進むさま。また、物事をためらわずに進めるさま。

nā nā なあなあ

nā nā
Describes carrying something out through collusion or compromise.

なあなあ
なれあい、妥協ですませること。また、その様子。

naga naga ながなが

naga naga
Describes something that is prolonged. Drawn-out. Lengthy. Often used to describe a speech that goes on longer than necessary. ☆*nagai*

ながなが
いかにも長いさま。話などが、必要以上に長たらしい様子。
☆長い

nayo nayo なよなよ

nayo nayo
Describes someone or something that is weak. Delicate. Supple.

なよなよ
しなやかで弱々しいさま。

niko niko
Describes someone smiling happily. All smiles.

にこにこ
うれしそうにほほえむさま。

niya niya にゃにゃ

niya niya
Describes smiling in a faint, meaningful manner. Grinning.

にやにや
意味ありげに薄笑いする様子。

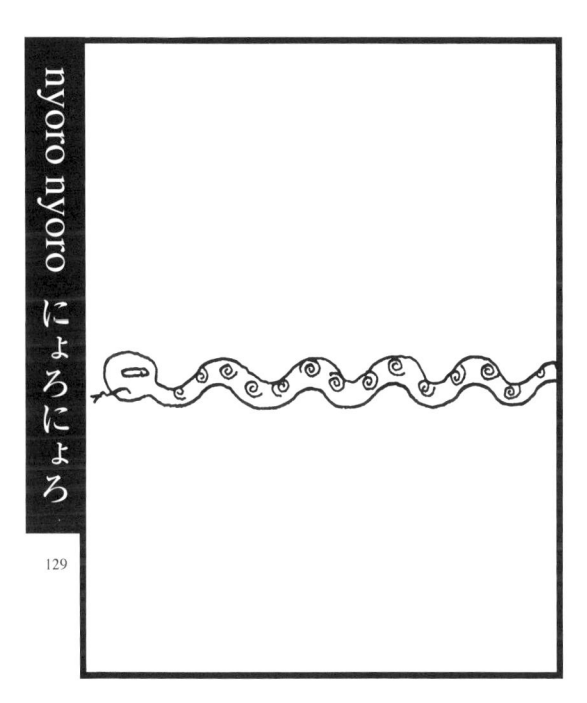

nyoro nyoro
Describes something long and thin, like a snake, moving along with a wriggling motion.

にょろにょろ
細長いものが身をくねらせて進むさま。

nuku nuku ぬくぬく

nuku nuku
①Describes having a feeling of warmth and comfort. Snugly. Cosily. ②Describes someone having an easy, carefree time.

ぬくぬく
①暖かく心地よいさま。②何の苦労もせず、いい思いをしている様子。

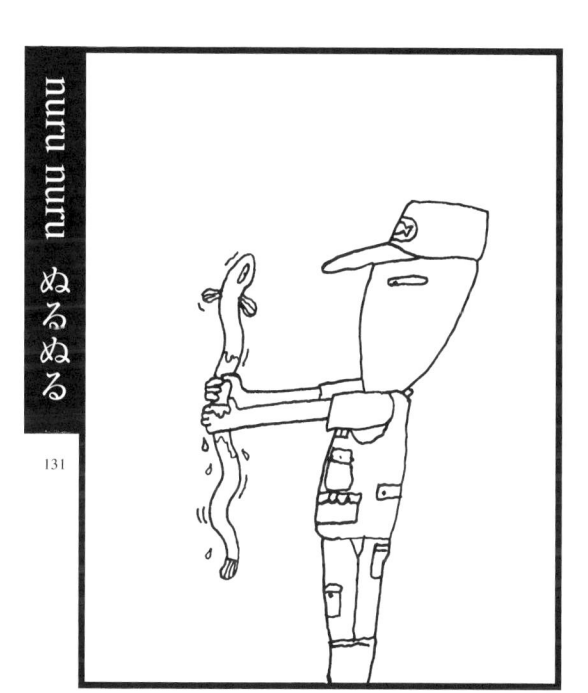

nuru nuru
Describes something slimy and slippery.

ぬるぬる
表面にぬめりがあって滑りやすいさま。また、そのもの。

nechi nechi
①Describes something sticky. Gluey. ②Describes tenacious character, behavior, or speech. Persistent.

ねちねち
①しつこく粘りつくさま。②性格や言動がしつこいさま。

neba neba ねばねば

neba neba
Describes something that is sticky and clings easily.
☆*nebaru*

ねばねば
粘りけがあって他のものにくっつきやすいさま。また、そのもの。☆粘る

noko noko のこのこ

noko noko
Describes someone appearing at a place quite nonchalantly, when he or she should really feel ashamed. Shamelessly. Casually. Unknowingly.

のこのこ
来ては具合が悪いはずの場に、平気で、あるいは何も知らずに出てくる様子。

noso noso のそのそ

noso noso
Describes moving slowly, clumsily. Often used to describe the movement of large people and animals. Lumbering.

のそのそ
動きが鈍いさま。体が大きい人や動物の動きを表すことが多い。

nobi nobi
Describes doing something in an easy and relaxed manner. Describes someone relaxing without any interruptions or worries. Leisurely. Expansive.
☆*nobiru* ※A homonym of this word describes something postponed many times. Put off again and again.

のびのび
自由でゆったりとしたさま。邪魔なものや心配事がなく、くつろいだ様子。☆伸びる ※べつに、何度も延期される様子を表す同音異義語「のびのび（延び延び）」あり。

noro noro
Describes moving slowly. Sluggishly. ☆*noroi*

のろのろ
動きがおそく、鈍いさま。☆のろい

haki haki
Describes speaking clearly or behaving with alacrity. Lucidly.

はきはき
言葉や態度が明確で歯切れよいさま。

paku paku
Describes someone opening and closing their mouth many times. Often used to describe someone eating heartily or a flap that keeps opening and closing.

ぱくぱく
口を大きく何度も開閉するさま。食べ方がさかんな様子や、物の合わせ目が開いたり閉じたりする様子などに用いる。

bata bata   ばたばた

bata bata
①Describes the sound of a flag or banner flapping in the wind. Fluttering. Also describes making a sound by shaking such objects. ②Describes objects falling down in succession. Also describes things taking place in rapid succession. ③Describes someone in a rush.

ばたばた
①布や板状のものが風にはためいたり打ち当たったりする音。また、それらを小刻みに動かして音を立てるさま。②物が次々に倒れるさま。また、物事が立て続けに行われる様子。③あわただしくふるまう様子。

hara hara
①Describes being anxious about how things are going to turn out. Apprehensive. ②Describes petals or tears falling gently. Trickling down.

はらはら
①事のなりゆきを心配して、気づかう様子。②花びら、涙などが少しずつ静かに落ちるさま。

bara bara ばらばら

bara bara
①Describes the sound of hailstones or acorns falling to the ground. ②Describes things scattered about or something that constituted a whole but has broken up. In bits and pieces. ③Describes something that lacks unity. Disjointed. In disorder.

ばらばら
①粒状のものが続けざまに落ちる音や様子。②散在するさま。また、ひとつにまとまっていたものが離れ離れになる様子。③物事に統一がとれていない様子。

bari bari
①Describes the act or the sound of tearing, chewing, or crunching something. ②Describes an energetic action. ③Describes something hard and stiff.

ばりばり
①厚みがあるものを力強く裂いたり噛んだり引っかいたりする音や様子。②物事を精力的にこなすさま。また、その人。③物が硬くこわばっているさま。

pika pika ぴかぴか

144

pika pika
Describes something sparkling. Glittering. Shining. Also used to describe something that is brand-new.

ぴかぴか
光り輝くさま。また、ま新しい様子を比喩的に言うこともある。

hiku hiku ひくひく

hiku hiku
Describes light convulsions in part of the body. Twitching.

ひくひく
体の一部などがかすかにけいれんする様子。

biku biku びくびく

①Describes part of the body shaking gently. Trembling. ②Describes someone who is afraid or nervous. Scared.

びくびく
①体の一部などが小刻みに震え動く様子。②恐怖や不安におびえるさま。

bisho bisho

Describes someone or something that is sopping wet. Soaking. Wet through.

びしょびしょ
雨や水にひどく濡れたさま。

hiso hiso
Describes talking so that others cannot hear. Whispering. Speaking in a hushed voice. ☆*hisokada*

ひそひそ
他人に聞かれないように、小声で話す様子。☆ひそかだ

hiya hiya
Describes being very frightened because of danger of uncertainty. Scared half to death. Terrified.
☆*hiyasu*

ひやひや
危険や不安を感じて、気が気でない様子。☆冷やす

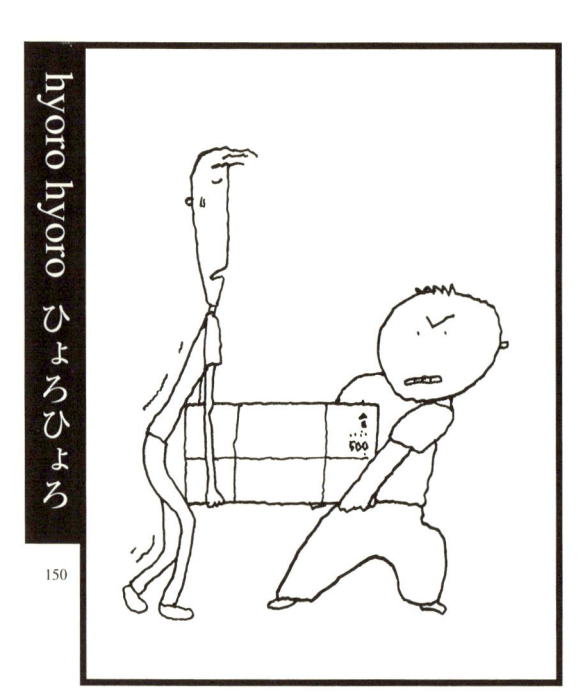

hyoro hyoro
Describes someone or something long and frail. Lanky. Also describes someone unsteady on their feet. Shaky. Swaying.

ひょろひょろ
細長く伸びて、か弱そうなさま。また、力なく足元がおぼつかない様子。

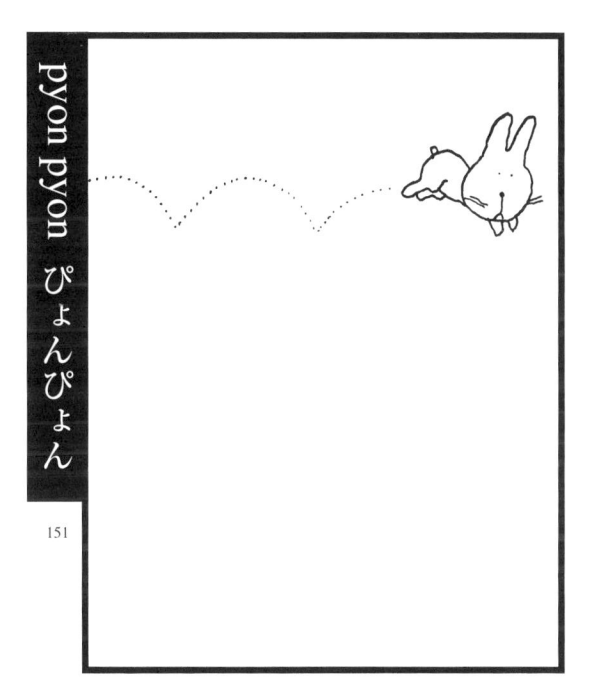

pyon pyon
Describes hopping or skipping agilely.

ぴょんぴょん
繰り返し、身軽にはねるさま。もっぱら、跳ぶ、はねるなどの形容に用いる。

hira hira ひらひら

hira hira
Describes objects like paper, a handkerchief, or petals falling. Fluttering. Swirling. Also used to describe a butterfly flying.

ひらひら
紙、布、花びらなど、薄くて軽いものがひるがえって揺れたり散ったりする様子。蝶が飛ぶ形容にも用いる。

hiri hiri ひりひり

hiri hiri
Describes stinging pain. Also used to describe a burning mouth after eating hot food.

ひりひり
皮膚に痛みなどの刺激を感じるさま。辛さが口の中を刺激するさまにも用いる。

biri biri びりびり

biri biri
①Describes the feeling one gets from an electric shock or the like. ②Describes the sound or act of tearing something up forcefully. Ripping. ③Describes the sound of something vibrating, such as a glass window rattled by a strong wind.

びりびり
①電気ショックなどで体がしびれる様子。また、そのような刺激を感じるさま。②紙、布などを勢いよく引き裂く音や様子。③物が小刻みに振動して出す音。また、その音が響くさま。爆風を受けた窓ガラスの音など。

buku buku

①Describes something outrageously fat. Flabby. Obese. ②Describes the sound or act of bubbles or foam rising or of something giving off bubbles while sinking. Also used to describe the sound of gargling.

ぶくぶく
①しまりなく太ったさま。②泡立つ音や様子。泡を出しながら沈んでいくさま、うがいをするさまにも用いる。

butsu butsu

①Describes muttering in a small voice. ②Describes complaining. Grumbling. ③Describes something with many small holes or lumps. Rash. ④Describes continuously piercing or cutting something into small pieces.

ぶつぶつ
①小声でつぶやくさま。②不平を言うさま。③小さな穴や突起がたくさんあるさま。また、そのもの。④何度も突き刺したり、短く切ったりするさま。

bura bura

①Describes a rather heavy object that is dangling and swaying. ②Describes walking without any real purpose or walking slowly. Strolling. ③Describes spending time without any proper job or schedule. Loafing around. Drifting through life.

ぶらぶら
①やや重いものが垂れ下がって揺れ動く様子。②さしたる目的もなく歩くさま。また、ゆっくり歩くさま。③決まった仕事や日課がなく、漫然と過ごすさま。

buru buru ぶるぶる

buru buru
Describes something shaking. Trembling. Also used to describe someone's body shaking from cold or fear. Shivering. Quaking.

ぶるぶる
小刻みに振動するさま。また、寒さや恐怖で体が震えるさま。

und und / ぷんぷん

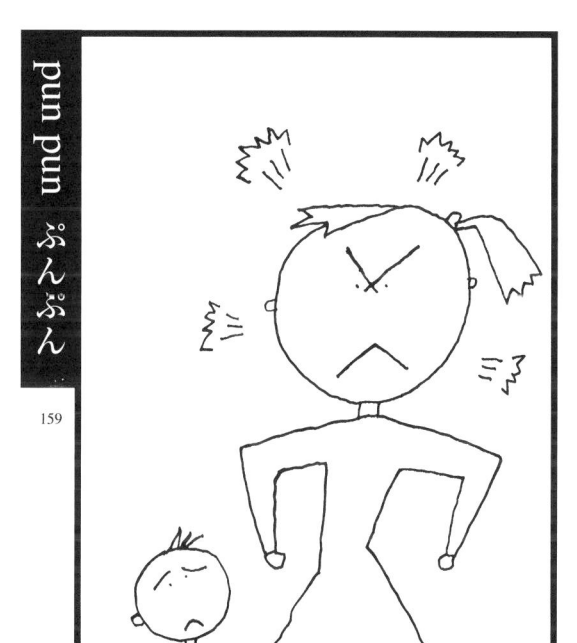

pun pun

①Describes someone who is very angry. ②Describes a strong smell hanging over a place.

ぷんぷん
①ひどく怒っているさま。怒りちらすさま。②強いにおいが立ちこめる様子。

peko peko ぺこぺこ

①Describes the sound or act of a thin sheet of metal or plastic being bent back and forth. Twanging. ②Describes bowing humbly many times and assuming a servile attitude. ③Describes being very hungry. Famished. Ravenous.

ぺこぺこ
①薄い金属板などがへこんだり、もとに戻ったりする音や様子。②何度も頭を下げるさま。何かにつけて下手(したて)に出て、こびへつらうさま。③ひどく空腹なさま。

beta beta

①Describes something sticky or clingy. ②Describes someone clinging to anothers. Often used to describe a man and woman who stick closely together. ③Describes covering a surface with paint, pieces of paper, or signatures.

べたべた
①粘りつくさま。②まとわりつくさま。とくに、男女がやたらにくっつき合う形容によく用いる。③一面をおおうように、塗りつけたり、いくつも紙を貼ったり、判を押したりする様子。

heto heto
へとへと

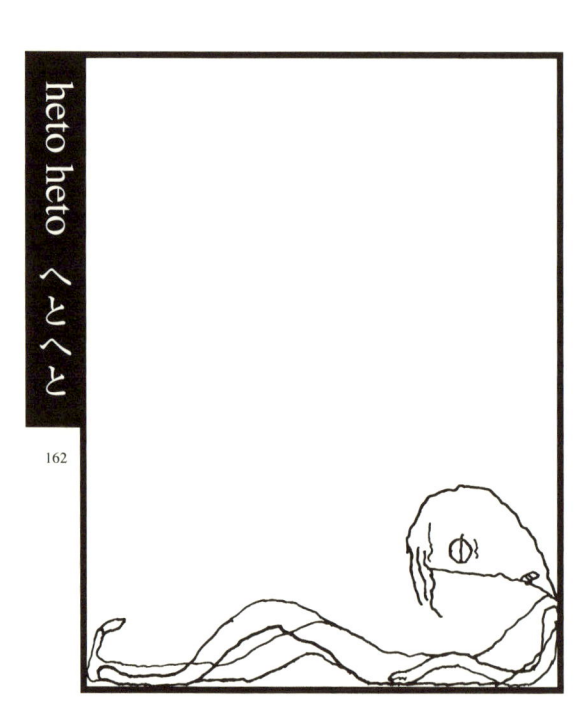

heto heto
Describes being so tired that one has no strength left. Exhausted. Pooped out.

へとへと
体じゅうの力が抜けるほど、ひどく疲れ切った様子。

hena hena へなへな

①Describes curving or bending. ②Describes someone becoming weak through loss of mental or physical strength. Buckling under. Ready to drop.

へなへな
①曲がったりしなったりするさま。②気力や体力がなくなったり弱まったりするさま。

hera hera へらへら

hera hera
Describes laughing frivolously or ambiguously. Also used to describe frivolous speech and behavior.

へらへら
意味もなく軽薄に笑うさま。あいまいに笑うさま。また、言動が軽々しい様子。

bera bera べらべら

bera bera
Describes speaking endlessly. Wagging one's tongue. Especially used to describe someone who goes so far as to say something they should not.

べらべら
とめどなくしゃべりまくるさま。とくに、言うべきではないことまでしゃべる様子によく用いる。

pera pera
①Describes chattering away frivolously. Glibly.
②Describes speaking fluently in a foreign language.
③Describes leafing through a book. Thumbing through. ④Describes cloth or wooden boards that are thin and cheap-looking.

ぺらぺら
①軽薄によくしゃべるさま。②外国語を流暢(りゅうちょう)に話すさま。③本などを続けてめくるさま。④布、板などが薄くて安っぽいさま。

pero pero ぺろぺろ

pero pero
Describes putting the tongue out and moving it around. Licking.

ぺろぺろ
舌を出して、さかんに動かすさま。舌でなめ回すさま。

hoka hoka ほかほか

hoka hoka
Describes something warm, especially warm, delicious-looking food. Steaming hot.

ほかほか
温かいさま。とくに、食べ物が湯気が立つほど温かくておいしそうな形容によく用いる。

poka poka
①Describes a feeling of warmth throughout one's body. ②Describes the sound or act of beating someone. Thumping.

ぽかぽか
①体の中まで暖かく気持ちいい様子。②続けざまに殴る音や様子。

bosa bosa
Describes unkempt, ruffled hair. Also used to describe the ragged tip of a broom or paintbrush.

ぼさぼさ
髪が乱れているさま。箒(ほうき)や筆などの毛先が不揃いな様子にも用いる。

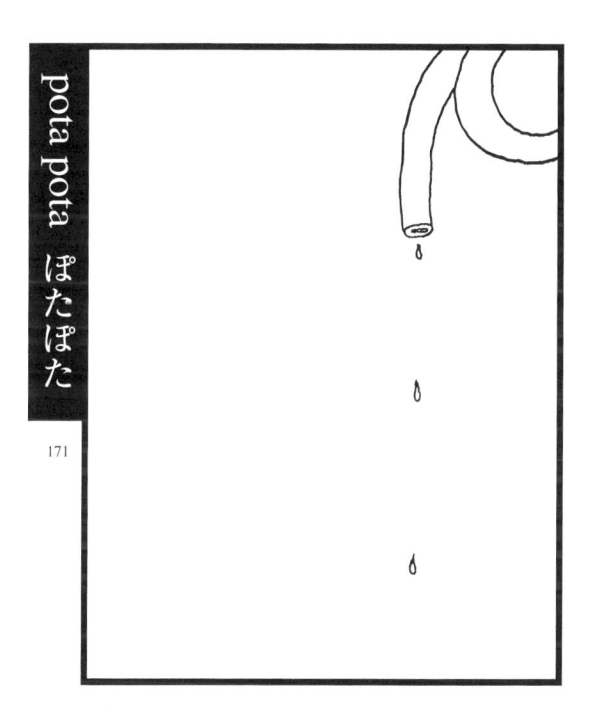

pota pota
Describes dripping water.

ぽたぽた
液体がしたたり落ちるさま。

hoya hoya ほやほや

hoya hoya
Describes something new or fresh, such as a newly wed couple or a new employee.

ほやほや
できたて、生まれたての状態。また、ある状態になって間もないさま。新婚や新入社員などの形容によく用いる。

boro boro ぼろぼろ

boro boro
①Describes something badly damaged. Also describes being mentally and physically worn-out. ②Describes falling grains. Also describes something that has lost its cohesion and crumbled. ③Describes wrongdoings or lies that are uncovered one after another.

ほろぼろ
①物がひどく傷んだ様子。また、心身が疲れ切ったさま。②粒状のものが次々にこぼれ落ちるさま。また、水分や粘りけがなくなって、粒々が離れ離れになった様子。③悪事やうそなどが次々に露見するさま。

maji maji
Describes taking a long, hard look at something. Staring.

まじまじ
じっと見つめるさま。視線をそらさず見据えるさま。もっぱら、見る形容に用いる。

mada mada
①Describes still having some way to go before reaching the goal. Short of the mark. ②Describes more of something to come, such as more reasons or more food. ☆*mada*

まだまだ
①ある状態・程度・段階に達するにはほど遠いさま。②同じような事柄がその他にもたくさんあるさま。☆まだ

machi machi
まちまち

machi machi
Describes things that are different. Diverse. Often used to describe things that could easily be the same but actually differ from one another. Varied.

まちまち
それぞれ異なる様子。同じでよいと思われるものが、ひとつひとつ違う場合に用いることが多い。

mie mie
Describes seeing through another person's scheme, especially lies or flattery. ☆*mieru*

みえみえ
相手の意図、とくに、うそやお世辞などが見えすいているさま。☆見える

muka muka
①Describes feeling sick. Queasy. ②Describes a surge of anger.

むかむか
①吐き気がするさま。②怒りがこみあげてくるさま。

mushi mushi
Describes hot, humid weather. Muggy. ☆*musu*

むしむし
湿度が高く、暑いさま。☆蒸す

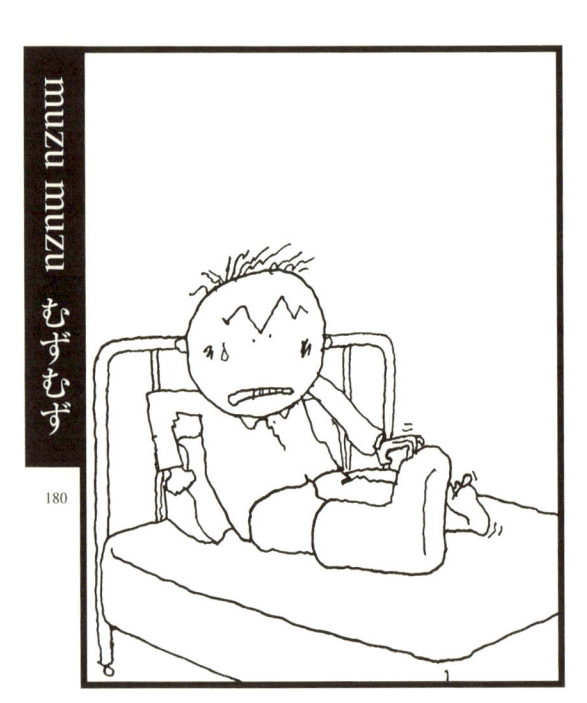

muzu muzu
①Describes an itchy feeling. Ticklish. ②Describes being impatient at not being able to do something one wants to do.

むずむず
①虫がはうようなかゆみを感じるさま。②何かをしたいのにできなくて、落ち着かない様子。はがゆいさま。

munya munya むにゃむにゃ

Describes muttering something meaningless. Often used to describe sleep talking.

むにゃむにゃ
わけのわからないことを口の中でつぶやく様子。また、寝言を言うさま。もっぱら、言う形容に用いる。

mun mun
Describes a stuffy or crowded atmosphere. Also used to describe a woman's or group of women's amorousness.

むんむん
熱気や人いきれがいっぱいに充満している様子。女性の色気が立ちこめるさまにも用いる。

meki meki
Describes progressing or growing rapidly and visibly. Conspicuously.

めきめき
進歩、成長などが目立って速いさま。

meso meso めそめそ

meso meso
Describes uncontrolled weeping. Sobbing. Also describes an effeminate man crying endlessly.

めそめそ
弱々しく泣くさま。すぐ涙ぐんだり、いつまでも泣いたりして女々しい様子。もっぱら、泣く形容に用いる。

moji moji もじもじ

185

moji moji
Describes someone behaving nervously or bashfully and unable to do what they want to do. Hesitantly.

もじもじ
遠慮したり恥ずかしがったりして、したいことができずにためらっているさま。

mota mota
Describes behavior or actions that are slow and inefficient. Clumsy.

もたもた
動作や物事の進行がのろくて、要領を得ない様子。

mori mori
①Describes something that rises powerfully. Swells.
②Describes someone full of zest or someone acting zestfully. Full of gusto. ☆*moru*

もりもり
①力強く盛り上がるさま。②意欲、元気などがさかんにわきおこるさま。また、意欲的、精力的に物事を行う様子。
☆盛る

mon mon
Describes someone worrying about something for a long time but unable to find a solution. In anguish.
※Always followed by *to*.

もんもん
ひどく悩み苦しむさま。深く思い悩んでも解決の糸口が見つからず、長時間苦しみ続ける様子。※つねに末尾に「と」を伴って用いる。

yasu yasu
Describes doing something with ease. Without difficulty. Effortlessly. ☆*yasui*

やすやす
いかにも簡単そうに。たやすく。☆やすい

yū yū
ゆうゆう

yū yū
Describes behaving confidently. Calmly. With plenty of leeway.

ゆうゆう
あわてず落ち着いているさま。充分余裕があるさま。

yusa yusa

Describes the swaying of something large and heavy, such as a tree. ☆*yusaburu*

ゆさゆさ

大きなもの、重いものがゆっくり大きく揺れる様子。もっぱら、揺れる，揺するなどの形容に用いる。☆揺さぶる

yura yura ゆらゆら

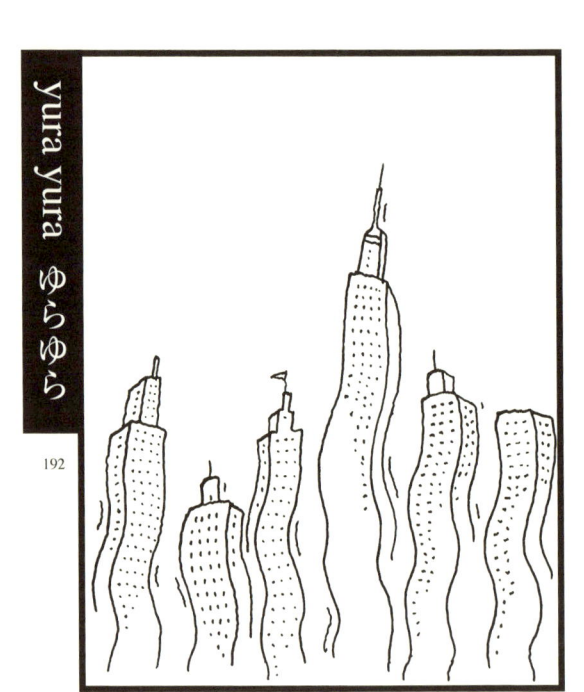

yura yura
Describes slow swaying. Swinging. Rolling. Wobbling.

ゆらゆら
ゆるやかに揺れ動くさま。もっぱら、揺れる形容に用いる。

yuru yuru

①Describes something very loose. ②Describes slow movement. ☆*yurui*

ゆるゆる
①とてもゆるいさま。ゆるんださま。②急がずゆっくり動くさま。☆ゆるい

yobo yobo
よぼよぼ

yobo yobo
Describes something weak and unsteady from old age.

よぼよぼ
年老いて、見るからに体力がなかったり足元がおぼつかなかったりする様子。

yoro yoro よろよろ

yoro yoro
Describes something unsteady on its feet and unstable. Tottering.

よろよろ
足取りが乱れて、体が不安定なさま。

rō rō

Describes singing or reciting in a loud, clear voice.
※Always followed by *to*.

ろうろう
声が大きく、澄みわたったさま。もっぱら、歌う、吟ずるなどの形容に用いる。※つねに末尾に「と」を伴う。

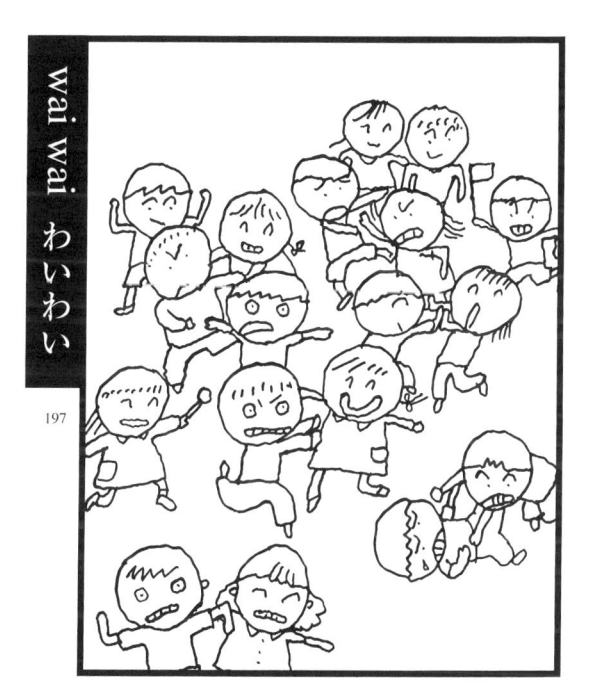

wai wai
Describes a large number of people behaving boisterously. Making a din.

わいわい
大勢が大声で騒ぐさま。

waku waku わくわく

waku waku
Describes someone who is bursting with excitement in anticipation of something. Thrilled.

わくわく
期待やうれしさで、胸がおどる様子。

waza waza
①Describes doing something on purpose, even though there is no need to. ②Describes doing something specially rather than incidentally.
☆*wazato*

わざわざ
①そうする必然性がないのに、故意にするさま。②何かのついでではなく、そのためだけにするさま。特別に。☆わざと

wan wan

① Describes a dog's bark. Bowwow. ②A child's word for a dog. *Incidentally, a cat mews *nyā nyā*, a cow moos *mō mō*, a pig oinks *bū bū*, a goat bleats *mē mē*, a crow caws *kā kā*, a sparrow tweets *chun chun*, and a frog croaks *kero kero*, and a fish goes...... ?

わんわん
①犬の泣き声。②幼児語で、犬そのもの。*ちなみに、ねこは「にゃあにゃあ」、牛は「もうもう」、ぶたは「ぶうぶう」、やぎは「めえめえ」、からすは「かあかあ」、すずめは「ちゅんちゅん」、かえるは「けろけろ」、さかなは……？

ALPHABETICAL LISTING

A
appu appu — 20
atsu atsu — 19

B
bara bara — 142
bari bari — 143
bata bata — 140
bera bera — 165
beta beta — 161
biku biku — 146
biri biri — 154
bisho bisho — 147
boro boro — 173
bosa bosa — 170
buku buku — 155
bura bura — 157
buru buru — 158
butsu butsu — 156

C
chibi chibi — 110
chiku chiku — 109
chira chira — 112
choko choko — 111

D
dabu dabu — 106
dara dara — 108
dere dere — 118
doki doki — 119
don don — 123
doro doro — 121

G
gabu gabu — 42
gaku gaku — 39
gami gami — 43
gatsu gatsu — 41
gaya gaya — 44
gera gera — 65
gira gira — 50
gisu gisu — 46
gocha gocha — 68
goso goso — 67
gowa gowa — 72
gucha gucha — 55
gui gui — 51
gun gun — 62
guru guru — 61
guzu guzu — 53
gyū gyū — 48

H
haki haki — 138
hara hara — 141
hena hena — 163

本書はあいうえお順レイアウトになっております。あいうえお順が不得意な方は、このABC順のリストをご利用下さい。

hera hera — 164	kan kan — 45
heto heto — 162	keba keba — 64
hiku hiku — 145	kechi kechi — 63
hira hira — 152	kibi kibi — 47
hiri hiri — 153	koro koro — 70
hiso hiso — 148	koso koso — 66
hiya hiya — 149	kotsu kotsu — 69
hoka hoka — 168	kowa gowa — 71
hoya hoya — 172	kudo kudo — 56
hyoro hyoro — 150	kune kune — 57
I	kura kura — 59
ichi ichi — 24	kuru kuru — 60
iji iji — 22	kusa kusa — 52
iki iki — 21	kuta kuta — 54
ira ira — 27	kuyo kuyo — 58
iso iso — 23	kyoro kyoro — 49
iya iya — 25	**M**
iyo iyo — 26	machi machi — 176
J	mada mada — 175
jabu jabu — 85	maji maji — 174
jiri jiri — 86	meki meki — 183
jiro jiro — 87	meso meso — 184
jito jito — 81	mie mie — 177
jiwa jiwa — 88	moji moji — 185
K	mon mon — 188
kachi kachi — 40	mori mori — 187

ALPHABETICAL LISTING

mota mota — 186
muka muka — 178
mun mun — 182
munya munya — 181
mushi mushi — 179
muzu muzu — 180

N
nā nā — 124
naga naga — 125
nayo nayo — 126
neba neba — 133
nechi nechi — 132
niko niko — 127
niya niya — 128
nobi nobi — 136
noko noko — 134
noro noro — 137
noso noso — 135
nuku nuku — 130
nuru nuru — 131
nyoro nyoro — 129

O
odo odo — 37
oro oro — 38
ota ota — 36
ozu ozu — 35

P
paku paku — 139
peko peko — 160
pera pera — 166
pero pero — 167
pika pika — 144
poka poka — 169
pota pota — 171
pun pun — 159
pyon pyon — 151

R
rō rō — 196

S
saba saba — 75
same zame — 77
samu zamu — 76
seka seka — 100
shā shā — 84
shibu shibu — 82
shige shige — 79
shiku shiku — 78
shimi jimi — 83
shizu shizu — 80
soro soro — 102
sowa sowa — 104
sugo sugo — 94

sui sui	89
suku suku	92
sura sura	97
sure sure	99
suya suya	96

T

taji taji	105
tara tara	107
teku teku	117
tobo tobo	120
ton ton	122
tsuka tsuka	113
tsun tsun	116
tsuru tsuru	115
tsuya tsuya	114

U

uda uda	32
uja uja	30
uji uji	29
uki uki	28
uro uro	34
uto uto	33
uzu uzu	31

W

wai wai	197
waku waku	198
wan wan	200
waza waza	199

Y

yasu yasu	189
yobo yobo	194
yoro yoro	195
yū yū	190
yura yura	192
yuru yuru	193
yusa yusa	191

Z

zā zā	73
zaku zaku	74
zoku zoku	101
zoro zoro	103
zuka zuka	90
zuke zuke	93
zuki zuki	91
zuru zuru	98
zuta zuta	95

その他の おもな重ね言葉 一覧

A List of Other Commonly Used Japanese Repeated Words.

あ
	あおあお	ao ao
	あかあか	aka aka
	あきあき	aki aki
	あとあと	ato ato
	あらあら	ara ara
	ありあり	ari ari
	あれあれ	are are

い
	いがいが	iga iga
	いちゃいちゃ	icha icha

う
	うかうか	uka uka
	うすうす	usu usu
	うつうつ	utsu utsu
	うつらうつら	utsura utsura
	うねうね	une une
	うはうは	uha uha
	うようよ	uyo uyo
	うんうん	un un

え
	えっさえっさ	essa essa
	えんえん	en en

お
	おいおい	oi oi
	おさおさ	osa osa
	おせおせ	ose ose
	おそるおそる	osoru osoru
	おちおち	ochi ochi
	おめおめ	ome ome
	おやおや	oya oya
	おりおり	ori ori
	おんおん	on on

か
	かさかさ	kasa kasa
	がさがさ	gasa gasa
	かしゃかしゃ	kasha kasha
	がしゃがしゃ	gasha gasha
	かすかす	kasu kasu
	かずかず	kazu kazu
	かたかた	kata kata
	がたがた	gata gata
	がたんがたん	gatan gatan
	がちがち	gachi gachi
	かちゃかちゃ	kacha kacha
	がちゃがちゃ	gacha gacha
	かちんかちん	kachin kachin
	かつかつ	katsu katsu
	がっぽがっぽ	gappo gappo
	かねがね	kane gane
	がばがば	gaba gaba
	がぼがぼ	gabo gabo
	からから	kara kara
	がらがら	gara gara
	からんからん	karan karan
	かりかり	kari kari
	がりがり	gari gari
	かるがる	karu garu

	がんがん	gan gan	
き	きいきい	kii kii	
	ぎいぎい	gii gii	
	ぎこぎこ	giko giko	
	ぎざぎざ	giza giza	
	きしきし	kishi kishi	
	ぎしぎし	gishi gishi	
	きちきち	kichi kichi	
	ぎちぎち	gichi gichi	
	きちんきちん	kichin kichin	
	きつきつ	kitsu kitsu	
	ぎとぎと	gito gito	
	きゃあきゃあ	kyā kyā	
	ぎゃあぎゃあ	gyā gyā	
	きゃっきゃっ	kyak kya(k)	
	きゃぴきゃぴ	kyapi kyapi	
	きゅっきゅっ	kyuk kyu(k)	
	きょときょと	kyoto kyoto	
	ぎょろぎょろ	gyoro gyoro	
	きらきら	kira kira	
	きりきり	kiri kiri	
	ぎりぎり	giri giri	
	ぎろぎろ	giro giro	
	ぎんぎん	gin gin	
く	くうくう	kū kū	
	ぐうぐう	gū gū	
	ぐさぐさ	gusa gusa	
	くしゃくしゃ	kusha kusha	
	ぐしゃぐしゃ	gusha gusha	
	ぐしょぐしょ	gusho gusho	
	くすくす	kusu kusu	
	くだくだ	kuda kuda	

ぐたぐた	guta guta	
ぐだぐだ	guda guda	
ぐちぐち	guchi guchi	
くちゃくちゃ	kucha kucha	
ぐちゅぐちゅ	guchu guchu	
ぐちょぐちょ	gucho gucho	
くっくっ	kuk ku(k)	
ぐつぐつ	gutsu gutsu	
ぐでんぐでん	guden guden	
くにゃくにゃ	kunya kunya	
ぐにゃぐにゃ	gunya gunya	
ぐびぐび	gubi gubi	
ぐらぐら	gura gura	
くりくり	kuri kuri	
ぐりぐり	guri guri	
くるんくるん	kurun kurun	
ぐるんぐるん	gurun gurun	
くろぐろ	kuro guro	
くんくん	kun kun	

け	げこげこ	geko geko
	げそげそ	geso geso
	けたけた	keta keta
	げたげた	geta geta
	けちょんけちょん	kechon kechon
	けらけら	kera kera
	げろげろ	gero gero
こ	こうこう	kō kō
	ごうごう	gō gō
	ごきごき	goki goki
	ごくごく	goku goku
	ごしごし	goshi goshi

	こせこせ	kose kose	
	ごたごた	gota gota	
	こちこち	kochi kochi	
	こちょこちょ	kocho kocho	
	ごちょごちょ	gocho gocho	
	こっくりこっくり	kokkuri kokkuri	
	ごつごつ	gotsu gotsu	
	ごつんごつん	gotsun gotsun	
	ごてごて	gote gote	
	こてんこてん	koten koten	
	ことこと	koto koto	
	ごとごと	goto goto	
	ごとんごとん	goton goton	
	こなごな	kona gona	
	ごにょごにょ	gonyo gonyo	
	こねこね	kone kone	
	ごぼごぼ	gobo gobo	
	ごほんごほん	gohon gohon	
	こまごま	koma goma	
	ごみごみ	gomi gomi	
	こりこり	kori kori	
	こりごり	kori gori	
	ごりごり	gori gori	
	ごろごろ	goro goro	
	ころんころん	koron koron	
	ごろんごろん	goron goron	
	こんこん	kon kon	
	ごんごん	gon gon	
さ	さあさあ	sā sā	
	さくさく	saku saku	
	ざっくざっく	zakku zakku	
	ざっくりざっくり	zakkuri zakkuri	
	ざっざっ	zaz za(z)	
	ざぶざぶ	zabu zabu	
	ざぶんざぶん	zabun zabun	
	さまざま	sama zama	
	さやさや	saya saya	
	さらさら	sara sara	
	ざらざら	zara zara	
	さわさわ	sawa sawa	
	ざわざわ	zawa zawa	
	さんさん	san san	
	ざんざん	zan zan	
し	じいじい	jii jii	
	しかじか	shika jika	
	じきじき	jiki jiki	
	じくじく	jiku jiku	
	しこしこ	shiko shiko	
	しとしと	shito shito	
	しなしな	shina shina	
	しましま	shima shima	
	しめしめ	shime shime	
	じめじめ	jime jime	
	じゃあじゃあ	jā jā	
	しゃかしゃか	shaka shaka	
	じゃかじゃか	jaka jaka	
	しゃきしゃき	shaki shaki	
	しゃなりしゃなり	shanari shanari	
	じゃらじゃら	jara jara	
	しゃりしゃり	shari shari	
	じゃりじゃり	jari jari	
	しゃんしゃん	shan shan	

	じゃんじゃん	jan jan	**せ** せいせい	sei sei
	しゅうしゅう	shū shū	ぜいぜい	zei zei
	じゅうじゅう	jū jū	ぜえぜえ	zē zē
	しゅるしゅる	shuru shuru	せっせせっせ	sesse sesse
	しゅんしゅん	shun shun		
	じょきじょき	joki joki	**そ** そうそう	sō sō
	しょぼしょぼ	shobo shobo	そこそこ	soko soko
	じょりじょり	jori jori	そよそよ	soyo soyo
	じょろじょろ	joro joro	そろりそろり	sorori sorori
	しらじら	shira jira		
	しらずしらず	shirazu shirazu	**た** たえだえ	tae dae
			たかだか	taka daka
	しわしわ	shiwa shiwa	だくだく	daku daku
	じわりじわり	jiwari jiwari	たびたび	tabi tabi
	しんしん	shin shin	たまたま	tama tama
	じんじん	jin jin	たんたん	tan tan
			だんだん	dan dan
す	すうすう	sū sū		
	すかすか	suka suka	**ち** ちかちか	chika chika
	ずきんずきん	zukin zukin	ちまちま	chima chima
	すけすけ	suke suke	ちゃかちゃか	chaka chaka
	ずしんずしん	zushin zushin	ちゃきちゃき	chaki chaki
	すたすた	suta suta	ちゃくちゃく	chaku chaku
	すっすっ	sus su(s)	ちゃぽちゃぽ	chapo chapo
	すぱすぱ	supa supa	ちゃらちゃら	chara chara
	ずばずば	zuba zuba	ちゅうちゅう	chū chū
	ずぶずぶ	zubu zubu	ちょいちょい	choi choi
	すべすべ	sube sube	ちょきちょき	choki choki
	すみずみ	sumi zumi	ちょくちょく	choku choku
	ずらずら	zura zura	ちょぼちょぼ	chobo chobo
	するする	suru suru	ちょろちょろ	choro choro
	ずんずん	zun zun	ちょんちょん	chon chon
			ちりちり	chiri chiri
			ちりんちりん	chirin chirin

	ちろちろ	chiro chiro
	ちんちん	chin chin
つ	つうつう	tsū tsū
	つぎつぎ	tsugi tsugi
	つくづく	tsuku zuku
	つぶつぶ	tsubu tsubu
	つらつら	tsura tsura
て	てかてか	teka teka
	でかでか	deka deka
	でぶでぶ	debu debu
	てらてら	tera tera
	でんでん	den den
と	とうとう	tō tō
	どうどう	dō dō
	どかどか	doka doka
	とくとく	toku toku
	どくどく	doku doku
	とげとげ	toge toge
	とことこ	toko toko
	どさどさ	dosa dosa
	どしどし	doshi doshi
	どすどす	dosu dosu
	とつとつ	totsu totsu
	とびとび	tobi tobi
	どぼんどぼん	dobon dobon
	どやどや	doya doya
	とろとろ	toro toro
な	なくなく	naku naku
	なみなみ	nami nami

に	にじにじ	niji niji
	にたにた	nita nita
	にちゃにちゃ	nicha nicha
	にまにま	nima nima
	にゅるにゅる	nyuru nyuru
	にょきにょき	nyoki nyoki
ぬ	ぬけぬけ	nuke nuke
	ぬめぬめ	nume nume
	ぬらぬら	nura nura
ね	ねとねと	neto neto
の	のうのう	nō nō
	のしのし	noshi noshi
	のっしのっし	nosshi nosshi
は	はあはあ	hā hā
	はいはい	hai hai
	ぱかぱか	paka paka
	ばさばさ	basa basa
	ぱさぱさ	pasa pasa
	ばしばし	bashi bashi
	ばしゃばしゃ	basha basha
	はたはた	hata hata
	ぱたぱた	pata pata
	ぱちぱち	pachi pachi
	ばちゃばちゃ	bacha bacha
	はやばや	haya baya
	ぱらぱら	para para
	ぱりぱり	pari pari
	はればれ	hare bare
	ばんばん	ban ban
	ぱんぱん	pan pan

ひ	ひいひい	hii hii	ふ	ふうふう	fū fū
	びいびい	bii bii		ぷうぷう	pū pū
	ぴいぴい	pii pii		ふかふか	fuka fuka
	ひえびえ	hie bie		ふかぶか	fuka buka
	ぴくぴく	piku piku		ぶかぶか	buka buka
	ぴこぴこ	piko piko		ぷかぷか	puka puka
	ひしひし	hishi hishi		ぷくぷく	puku puku
	びしびし	bishi bishi		ふさふさ	fusa fusa
	ぴしぴし	pishi pishi		ぶすぶす	busu busu
	ひたひた	hita hita		ふつふつ	futsu futsu
	ぴたぴた	pita pita		ぶつぶつ	putsu putsu
	ぴちぴち	pichi pichi		ふにゃふにゃ	funya funya
	びちゃびちゃ	bicha bicha		ぶよぶよ	buyo buyo
	ぴちゃぴちゃ	picha picha		ふらふら	fura fura
	びちょびちょ	bicho bicho		ぶりぶり	buri buri
	ひゃらひゃら	hyara hyara		ぷりぷり	puri puri
	ひゅうひゅう	hyū hyū		ぷりんぷりん	purin purin
	びゅうびゅう	byū byū		ぶるんぶるん	burun burun
	ぴゅうぴゅう	pyū pyū		ふわふわ	fuwa fuwa
	ひゅるひゅる	hyuru hyuru		ふんふん	fun fun
	びゅんびゅん	byun byun		ぶんぶん	bun bun
	ひょいひょい	hyoi hyoi			
	ひょうひょう	hyō hyō	へ	ぺいぺい	pei pei
	ひょこひょこ	hyoko hyoko		ぺかぺか	peka peka
	ぴょこぴょこ	pyoko pyoko		へこへこ	heko heko
	ぴよぴよ	piyo piyo		べこべこ	beko beko
	びらびら	bira bira		へたへた	heta heta
	ぴらぴら	pira pira		ぺたぺた	peta peta
	ぴりぴり	piri piri		べちゃべちゃ	becha becha
	ひろびろ	hiro biro		ぺちゃぺちゃ	pecha pecha
	ひんひん	hin hin		べとべと	beto beto
	びんびん	bin bin		ぺとぺと	peto peto
	ぴんぴん	pin pin		べりべり	beri beri
				へろへろ	hero hero

	べろべろ	bero bero		ぽろんぽろん	poron poron
	べろんべろん	beron beron		ぼんぼん	bon bon
	ぺんぺん	pen pen		ぽんぽん	pon pon
ほ	ほいほい	hoi hoi	ま	まあまあ	mā mā
	ぽいぽい	poi poi		まえまえ	mae mae
	ほうぼう	hō bō		まごまご	mago mago
	ほきほき	boki boki		まざまざ	maza maza
	ぽきぽき	poki poki		ますます	masu masu
	ほくほく	hoku hoku		まずまず	mazu mazu
	ぼこぼこ	boko boko		またまた	mata mata
	ぽこぽこ	poko poko		まるまる	maru maru
	ぼそぼそ	boso boso		まんまん	man man
	ぼたぼた	bota bota			
	ぼちぼち	bochi bochi	み	みいんみいん	miin miin
	ぽちぽち	pochi pochi		みしみし	mishi mishi
	ぼちゃぼちゃ	bocha bocha		みしりみしり	mishiri mishiri
	ぽちゃぽちゃ	pocha pocha		みすみす	misu misu
	ぼつぼつ	botsu botsu		みちみち	michi michi
	ぽつぽつ	potsu potsu		みなみな	mina mina
	ぽつんぽつん	potsun potsun		みゃくみゃく	myaku myaku
	ぼてぼて	bote bote		みりみり	miri miri
	ほとほと	hoto hoto		みるみる	miru miru
	ほどほど	hodo hodo			
	ぼとぼと	boto boto	む	むくむく	muku muku
	ぽとぽと	poto poto		むざむざ	muza muza
	ほのぼの	hono bono		むしゃむしゃ	musha musha
	ぼやぼや	boya boya		むちむち	muchi muchi
	ぼりぼり	bori bori		むらむら	mura mura
	ぽりぽり	pori pori			
	ほろほろ	horo horo	め	めためた	meta meta
	ぽろぽろ	poro poro			
	ぼろんぼろん	boron boron			

	めちゃめちゃ	mecha mecha		よたよた	yota yota
	めらめら	mera mera		よちよち	yochi yochi
	めりめり	meri meri		よれよれ	yore yore
	めろめろ	mero mero			
	めんめん	men men	**ら**	らくらく	raku raku
				らんらん	ran ran
も	もくもく	moku moku			
	もぐもぐ	mogu mogu	**り**	りいんりいん	riin riin
	もこもこ	moko moko		りゅうりゅう	ryū ryū
	もごもご	mogo mogo		りんりん	rin rin
	もしもし	moshi moshi			
	もしゃもしゃ	mosha mosha	**る**	るいるい	rui rui
				るんるん	run run
	もじゃもじゃ	moja moja			
	もそもそ	moso moso	**れ**	れろれろ	rero rero
	もぞもぞ	mozo mozo		れんれん	ren ren
	もてもて	mote mote			
	もともと	moto moto	**ろ**	ろくろく	roku roku
	もやもや	moya moya			
	もろもろ	moro moro	**わ**	わあわあ	wā wā
				わさわさ	wasa wasa
や	やあやあ	yā yā		わなわな	wana wana
	やいやい	yai yai			
	やいのやいの	yaino yaino			
	やまやま	yama yama			
	やれやれ	yare yare			
ゆ	ゆくゆく	yuku yuku			
	ゆめゆめ	yume yume			
よ	よいよい	yoi yoi			
	よくよく	yoku yoku			
	よしよし	yoshi yoshi			

本文辞書作成＊大山直美
英訳＊ジョン・タラント
本文デザイン＊ももはらるみこ

本作品は1989年12月、ジャパンタイムズより刊行された
『英語人と日本語人のための日本語擬態語辞典』を、文
庫収録にあたり一部加筆訂正し、再編集したものです。

五味太郎―1945年、東京都に生まれる。絵本作家。桑沢デザイン研究所ID科卒業。インダストリアルデザインから、絵本を中心とした創作活動に入り、300冊に及ぶ作品を発表。独創的な作風で幅広いファンを持ち、海外でも翻訳出版される。『かくしたのだあれ』『たべたのだあれ』(以上、文化出版局)でサンケイ児童出版文化賞、『ときどきの少年』(ブロンズ新社)で路傍の石文化賞、ボローニャ国際絵本原画展賞他、受賞多数。エッセイ、服飾デザイン、アニメーションビデオ制作などの分野でも活躍。著書には『さる・るるる』(絵本館)、『創作ことわざ絵本』(岩崎書店)、『ぼくはタイガースだBeing The Tigers.』(集英社)、『大人問題』(講談社文庫)『ここまできてそれなりにわかったこと』(講談社)などがある。

講談社+α文庫　日本語擬態語辞典(にほんごぎたいごじてん)

五味太郎(ごみたろう)　©Taro Gomi 2004

本書のコピー、スキャン、デジタル化等の無断複製は著作権法上での例外を除き禁じられています。本書を代行業者等の第三者に依頼してスキャンやデジタル化することは、たとえ個人や家庭内の利用でも著作権法違反です。

2004年6月20日第1刷発行
2016年12月1日第15刷発行

発行者	鈴木 哲
発行所	株式会社 講談社

東京都文京区音羽2-12-21 〒112-8001
電話　編集(03)5395-3532
　　　販売(03)5395-4415
　　　業務(03)5395-3615

装画	五味太郎
デザイン	鈴木成一デザイン室
カバー印刷	凸版印刷株式会社
印刷	慶昌堂印刷株式会社
製本	株式会社国宝社

落丁本・乱丁本は購入書店名を明記のうえ、小社業務あてにお送りください。送料は小社負担にてお取り替えします。
なお、この本の内容についてのお問い合わせは
第一事業局企画部「+α文庫」あてにお願いいたします。
Printed in Japan　ISBN4-06-256853-5
定価はカバーに表示してあります。

講談社+α文庫 Ⓑ ことば

書名	著者	内容	価格	番号
日本語擬態語辞典	五味太郎	日本が世界に誇るべき文化「擬態語」を、絵と英語で解説。感覚言語の真の姿が一目瞭然！	670円	B 47-1
3カ月で結果が出る！資格が取れる！「超効率」勉強法	高島徹治	53歳から90以上の試験に合格！ 最少時間で最大効果を引き出す32の体験的勉強法を公開	600円	B 51-3
みるみる身につく！イメージ英語革命	大西泰斗 ポール・クリス・マクベイ	暗記は不要！ イラスト＋語感＝イメージですっきりわかる、ネイティブ英語の学習法!!	850円	B 52-1
言ってはいけない！ 部下と上司の禁句	齋藤孝	自分を偉く見せるため、責任を回避するため発せられる上司のNGワードに対抗する方法	590円	B 53-3
＊「こいつは違う！」と言わせる仕事術	齋藤孝	仕事ができる人になるため、まずこのセリフを口に出せ！ 心と頭を鍛える37のマニュアル！	619円	B 53-4
＊つがわ式世界最速漢字記憶ドリル	津川博義	○をつけるだけでスイスイ難しい漢字が脳に入る驚異のつがわ式を役立つドリルで体験！	648円	B 64-1
世界最速「超」記憶法	津川博義	○をつけるだけで英単語も漢字もみるみる覚えられる。受験にも老後にも万能の記憶法！	600円	B 64-2
ハングルの愉快な迷宮	戸田郁子	韓国語学習歴30年の著者がハングルの奥深い世界を、愛情こめて描いた愉快エッセイ集！	743円	B 67-1
＊悩ましくて愛しいハングル	戸田郁子	韓国語と日本語。微妙な違いを生む生活習慣、歴史文化の違いを愛情こめて描いたエッセイ	600円	B 67-2
悩ましくて愛しいソウル大家族	戸田郁子	韓流のかけらもない'91年に韓国人写真家と結婚。家族主義と格闘する熱く楽しい日々！	848円	B 67-3

＊印は書き下ろし・オリジナル作品

表示価格はすべて本体価格（税別）です。本体価格は変更することがあります